Christian Worldview
For Children
Training the Heart and Mind of a Child
to Follow Christ

BRANNON HOWSE
President and Founder of Worldview Weekend

CHRISTIAN WORLDVIEW FOR CHILDREN
Published by Worldview Weekend Publishing
a division of Worldview Weekend

© 2006 by Brannon Howse
International Standard Book Number:
0-9785014-1-1

Cover Design by Steve Gamble

Unless noted otherwise, Scripture quotations are from
The Holy Bible, New King James Version (NKJV)
© 1994 by Thomas Nelson, Inc.

FOR INFORMATION:
WWW.WORLDVIEWWEEKEND.COM

PRINTED IN THE UNITED STATES OF AMERICA

DEDICATION

*T*his book is dedicated to my daughter Libby. I pray
that you, Libby, will grow in Godly knowledge and
wisdom, that your heart will seek God, and that your life
will reflect a strong commitment to Jesus Christ. As the
world becomes more and more evil and America becomes a
more hostile place for Christians to live, I pray that you will
be like a tree planted by the rivers of water, that brings forth
its fruit in its season, whose leaf also shall not wither; and
whatever you do shall prosper (Psalm 1:3).

Love,

Dad

September 1, 2006

ACKNOWLEDGMENTS

Thank you to my editor Greg Webster, to Bob Heyer for page layout, to Steve Gamble for cover design, and to Ray Comfort and Jeanne Howse for feedback on the manuscript.

TABLE OF CONTENTS

FOREWORD

The number one book that I recommend to parents who want to raise Godly children is the Bible. However, I am always on the lookout for resources to help me be a more effective and successful Christian parent to my three children. It is imperative that any book I read is deeply grounded in the Word of God, and it is because of this that I encourage you to read and re-read with your young ones *Christian Worldview for Children*. Brannon Howse's book fills a serious void and is an invaluable tool that will assist you to train the heart and mind of a child in the central Christian doctrines upon which they can build their own faith and life.

As you may know, I "grew up" on television as D. J. Tanner, the oldest daughter on the TV sitcom *Full House*. While still an early elementary-age child, I had to memorize my lines for an episode and then, just a few days later, memorize an entirely new script. I read and memorized thousands of pages. I also had to be on time, sit quietly for long periods waiting for my turn to be on camera, make dozens of public appearances each year, be sharp for media interviews and do my schoolwork. I was doing the job of an adult even though just a child. One reason I was successful as a young actress is because I loved the challenge.

Perhaps you have heard it said that kids are like sponges? Based on my experience, it is true. Often children can memorize and recall information faster than adults. Ask any elementary school boy who is a sports fan, and let him tell you about his favorite hockey team or baseball player. You'll feel the passion as the information spills forth. I've listened to a child present facts about this spider, that snake, or some other bug—all learned from watching *Animal Planet*. So why don't we expect more of our kids when it comes to their Biblical knowledge?

Most children truly like to be challenged and will get excited about the things which excite us. As a Christian parent, I know one of the most important things I can do is share with my children an excitement for and commitment to Biblical truth. By teaching essentials of our faith to my children, I prepare their hearts to seek God. *Christian Worldview for Children* is helping my husband and me accomplish this goal.

What could be more important than placing in the heart and mind of a child a deep conviction that Jesus Christ is God, that there are good reasons to believe He rose from the dead, that the Bible is a true and accurate revelation from beginning to end, that all have sinned and fallen short of the glory of God, that salvation is found only in and through Jesus Christ, that there is absolute truth for all time, people, and places? There are far too many deceptive worldviews vying for the heart and mind of your child, and only by training your child in Biblical truth will he or she be quick to reject the lies of the false worldviews that otherwise lead to destruction.

Teaching to the heart is vital if we want to grow up children who passionately seek and follow God. What Christian parent does not want that?

Thanks, Brannon, for writing this book, and thank you, Christian adult, for reading it to a child.

—Candace Cameron Buré

PREFACE

For Adults Who Want to Train the Heart and Mind
of a Child to Follow Jesus Christ

The Bible instructs parents to "train up a child in the way he should go, and when he is old he will not depart from it" (Proverbs 22:6).

I want to thank and commend you for using this book to teach a young person to follow Jesus Christ. While godly training is the most important responsibility of a parent, it is, as you have likely discovered, hard work. Training does not just happen by chance. It takes time, discipline, sacrifice, patience, and consistency.

In your hands is a Christian worldview primer for children—one I wrote because I could not find a book to use to give my own children the foundation for a Biblical worldview. Yet I knew if I were going to train my children to follow Jesus Christ, I needed to start early, and I knew the teaching must be specific. Since it is not obvious to everyone, let me explain for a moment why training the hearts *and* minds of our children to know the basics of our faith is so important.

The Bible Tells Me So

The Bible mentions the heart 826 times. "Heart" refers to the core of a person's being. Proverbs 4:23 says out of the heart "spring the issues of life." From the heart proceed our good and bad thoughts, emotions, and behavior. So, preparing the soil of a child's heart is crucial if we want to plant the seeds of Biblical truth and see them grow to maturity.

The Bible says we are to love the Lord our God with all our *heart*, soul, strength, and *mind*. Unfortunately, many Christians ignore this last point. Christianity is not something we believe by blind faith. There are solid reasons to become a Christian. Scripture variously commands us to think, reason, discern, judge, determine, contend, and argue—all activities of the mind. Using one's mind in service to Jesus Christ is an act of worship and love.

In Scripture, the words "heart" and "mind" are often interchangeable, and other times they complement one another. Jeremiah 17:9, for instance, describes the heart as "deceitful above all things, and desperately wicked," so the mind must moderate the heart. The Bible also describes the nature of those who ignore God and tells us how to practice godliness:

- Psalm 14:1, "The fool has said in his heart, 'There is no God.'"

- Proverbs 23:19, "Hear, my son, and be wise; And guide your heart in the way."

- Deuteronomy 4:9, "Only take heed to yourself, and diligently keep yourself, lest you forget the things your eyes have seen, and lest they depart from your heart all the days of your life."

- Matthew 12:35, "A good man out of the good treasure of his heart brings forth good things, and an evil man out of the evil treasure brings forth evil things."

- Proverbs 23:7, "For as he thinks in his heart, so is he."

Your heart and mind are part of your soul, the core of who you are—and who you will still be after you die. The heart and mind will live forever and be judged by God (Romans 2:5; Revelation 2:23). The person that repents of sin and surrenders his or her will to the Lordship of Jesus Christ is the person who has received mercy and grace. That person has been saved by God on the basis of

Christ's complete payment for sin at Calvary. In the day of destruction, the saved person is not judged because of his or her sins.

Training the heart and mind of a child to follow Jesus Christ is not just about this life, but also about the life to come. It is about *eternity*. Could there be any more important job for a Christian parent? Romans 10:10 says, "For with the heart one believes unto righteousness, and with the mouth confession is made unto salvation."

The Biblical Goals of Christian Training

Is this business of training just so our children will be well behaved and make us look good in public? Or is it so they will seek God? In his excellent book, *Shepherding a Child's Heart*, Tedd Tripp outlines why we must intently train our children:

> Therefore, your parenting goal cannot simply be well-behaved children...your concern is to unmask your child's sin, helping him to understand how it reflects a heart that has strayed. That leads to the cross of Christ. It underscores the need for a Savior.[1]

> The central focus of childrearing is to bring chil-

dren to a sober assessment of themselves as sinners. They must understand the mercy of God, who offered Christ as a sacrifice for sinners. How is that accomplished? You must address the heart as the fountain of behavior and the conscience as the God-given judge of right and wrong. The cross of Christ must be the central focus of your child-rearing... the focal point of your discipline and correction must be your children seeing their utter inability to do the things that God requires unless they know the help and strength of God.[2]

The vast necessity of training children can be summarized in five central goals for a Christian parent. We train our children so they will do these things:

1. Seek God
• Although King Jehoshaphat of Judah—according to 2 Chronicles 19:3—was not saved, he had taken steps to prepare his heart to seek God: he removed idols from his land. Just as the non-believing king prepared himself for God, we can prepare the hearts of our children early on to seek God by making sure they have no idols in the way.

2. **Acknowledge their sinfulness, repent, and follow Jesus Christ as Savior and Lord of their lives.**

- 1 Thessalonians 5:23, "…and may your whole spirit, soul, and body be preserved blameless at the coming of our Lord Jesus Christ."

3. **Live a life centered around pleasing God, not men, by doing His will *from the heart*, not as a legalistic compulsion.**

- Ephesians 6:6-7, "…as bondservants of Christ, doing the will of God from the heart, with goodwill doing service, as to the Lord, and not to men…"
- Romans 6:17, "…you obeyed from the heart that form of doctrine to which you were delivered…"
- Matthew 22:37, "Jesus said to him, "'You shall love the Lord your God with all your heart, with all your soul, and with all your mind." This is the first and great commandment.'"

4. **Fulfill the Great Commission: To make disciples who follow Jesus Christ.**

    • Ezra 7:10, "...For Ezra had prepared his heart to seek the Law of the Lord, and to do it, and to teach statutes and ordinances in Israel." Here is an example of preparing the heart to seek God and His laws and to teach them to others.

    • 1 Peter 3:15, "But sanctify the Lord God in your hearts, and always be ready to give a defense to everyone who asks you a reason for the hope that is in you, with meekness and fear..."

5. **Have a comprehensive Biblical worldview so as to understand the times and know what God would have them do.**

    • 1 Chronicles 12:32 tells us that in Israel there were men "who had understanding of the times, to know what Israel ought to do..."

How to Train the Heart/Mind of a Child

Unless our children know the Bible, they will not be thoroughly equipped for every good work. It is impossible to apply a Biblical worldview to our laws, science, economics, history, families, government, religion, and social issues unless we know the doctrines of Scripture.

Doctrine is all about the will of God and the Gospel—Jesus taught doctrine during His earthly ministry. To ignore doctrine is to ignore God's commandments, the teachings of Jesus Christ, and what the Bible reveals concerning salvation. In order for children to understand God, we must teach them the moral law, because moral law is a reflection of God's character and nature. Everything consistent with the character and nature of God is truth, and everything contrary is untruth.

Parents must connect the Word of God, the moral law, and Christian doctrine with the character and nature of God. It gives a very skewed picture simply to tell a child to do or not to do something ONLY because the Bible says so. The Bible "says so" because of God's nature. If we teach our children that the Bible is a book of rules for behavior, then we are leading them down the road to legalism and rebellion. Rather, we must be clear that the Word of God reveals God Himself. He wants us to model His character so we can bring honor and glory to Him, be witnesses to the unsaved, and enter a deeper relationship with Him.

As you train the heart and mind of your child, use the moral law to reveal to your child his or her inborn sinful and lost condition, to communicate the need for repentance, and to explain the grace and mercy of our holy and just God. The moral law reveals the disease as well as the need for the cure which is only found in salvation through Jesus Christ.

Remember: The purpose of our training is to prepare the soil of our children's hearts so they will seek God for themselves and be convicted of sinfulness and the need to repent. Forcing or coercing children to "pray a sinner's prayer" will not save them but only make false converts. I know this well from personal experience. At the age of five, I prayed a "sinner's prayer," and at seven I walked the aisle to join our church and be baptized. For years, I used these acts to affirm my salvation. I learned to "perform," to do what was expected of me, or to do what I knew would make other Christians respect and accept me.

I played the "game" even though I didn't know I was playing a game. I thought I was saved because I had prayed the right prayer, walked the aisle, and was baptized. It was not until I read *Revival's Golden Key* by Ray Comfort that I understood my total depravity and need for Biblical repentance. (Ray Comfort's book is now titled, *Way of the Master* and is available in our online bookstore at www. worldviewweekend.com). Ray reveals Biblical teachings about the moral law—the lost key to understanding why we need salvation. Subsequently, I worked out my salvation with "fear and trembling" and went from false to true conversion.

The Moral Law Is a Wake-up Call to Change Hearts and Minds—and Bring Repentance

According to Romans, the moral law is written on the heart and mind of every person—thus the conscience. "Con" means with and "science" means knowledge. So, every time people sin or rebel against God, they know it is wrong. We come to understand that we don't murder fellow human beings because murder goes against the character of God. We are not to lie, steal, or break any of the other Ten Commandments because doing so would go against who God is. Romans 1:21 reminds us, "although they knew God, they did not glorify Him as God, nor were thankful, but became futile in their thoughts, and their foolish hearts were darkened." And Romans 2:15 points out that people "show the work of the law written in their hearts, their conscience also bearing witness, and between themselves their thoughts accusing or else excusing them."

People can either accept the guilty feeling of the law that accuses them of their transgressions when they sin, or they can excuse the guilty feeling and learn to ignore it. If they ignore the guilt long enough or often enough, they will become people "speaking lies in hypocrisy, having their own conscience seared with a hot iron" (1 Timothy 4:2). Norm Geisler explains how this works out in a person's life:

> [T]he root cause of the character disorders (moral corruption) … is directly associated with a person's refusal to acknowledge and act upon what is morally right and reject what is morally wrong. It becomes harder and harder for the individual to get help with his character disorder because of the increased moral depravity. This increase is associated with greater levels of insensitivity in that person's conscience. For example, during the progressive moral deterioration in the life of the person who uses pornography, his sequence of feeling-to-thought-to-deed proceeds with less and less intervention of the inhibitory mechanism of conscience and guilt.[3]

This is the effect of having your conscience seared, but no one will have an excuse at judgment for rejecting

God. Romans 3:19–20 explains:

> Now we know that whatever the law says, it says
> to those who are under the law, that every mouth
> may be stopped, and all the world may become
> guilty before God. Therefore by the deeds of the
> law no flesh will be justified in His sight, for by
> the law is the knowledge of sin.

Everyone has broken the law. None can justify their entry into heaven by claiming they have "lived a good enough life," because God's standard is to keep the complete moral law, and no one has done that.

To further underscore that committing sin is breaking the moral law, 1 John 3:4 says, "Whoever commits sin also commits lawlessness, and sin is lawlessness." And Romans 3:10 explains, "There is none righteous, no, not one." Finally, Romans 3:23 concludes: "…all have sinned and fall short of the glory of God."

Because everyone but Jesus Christ has broken the law, any who have not repented of their sins and trusted in the death, burial, and resurrection of Jesus Christ will not be pardoned for breaking the moral law. To repent means to turn from sin, to stop practicing sin as a lifestyle. This does not mean you will never sin again, but there is a big difference between stumbling into sin and willingly jumping in. A repentant heart is born out of an awareness of your deep-seated sinfulness and the understanding that you deserve the wrath of God. Any repentant person who surrenders his or her life to Christ receives eternal life with Christ. Eternal life is given at the moment of salvation because Christ fully paid for the person's sin when He died in that person's place. Second Corinthians 7:9-10 says:

> Now I rejoice, not that you were made sorry, but that your sorrow led to repentance. For you were made sorry in a godly manner, that you might suffer loss from us in nothing. For godly sorrow produces repentance leading to salvation, not to be regretted; but the sorrow of the world pro-duces death.

True repentance is a "godly sorrow" for sin; it is turn-ing and going in the opposite direction of your willful sin-ful lifestyle. True repentance leads to a change in a person's life as he or she grows in relationship with Jesus Christ.

My friend Mark Cahill speaks for the Worldview Weekend and wrote an outstanding book entitled *One Thing You Can't Do in Heaven*. In his book, Mark offers a superb explanation of the real meaning and result of repentance:

One topic that I believe we must talk about when we discuss sin is repentance. It seems to be a word that we don't use much in witnessing, and a word that some people don't want to use at all. Yet the word "repent" and its various forms is used over one hundred times in the Bible. It must be a very important word then, and something that we must understand.

The apostle Paul tells us in 2 Corinthians 7:10, "For godly sorrow produces repentance to salvation, not to be regretted; but the sorrow of the world produces death."

John the Baptist preached in the wilderness, "Repent, for the kingdom of heaven is at hand!" (Matthew 3:2).

Jesus preached this same message of repentance. Mark 1:14, 15 says, "Now after John was put in prison, Jesus came to Galilee, preaching the gospel of the kingdom of God, and saying, 'The time is fulfilled, and the kingdom of God is at hand. Repent, and believe the gospel.'"

In Mark 6, Jesus sends out the twelve disciples two by two. Verse 12 states, "So they went out and preached that people should repent." If Jesus sent the disciples out preaching that people must repent of their sins, we ought to do the same.

Repentance is not when we feel bad because we got caught doing something wrong. True repentance is when we change our mind about our sin so our actions will not continue to be the same. . . .

I was sitting around talking one night with a young man I had met at a camp. He was telling me about his life and confessed that he had been using cocaine for the past thirty days. About forty-five minutes into the conversation he asked, "Is this the point where you are going to start talking to me about Jesus?"

I said, "No." He looked rather surprised. "You're not?" I told him that he was not ready for Jesus, and that it was not his day to get saved. He did not hate his sin enough to want to repent and walk away from it. He loved the world way too much. It was very interesting that he didn't argue one bit with me. He didn't want to get saved that day. He wanted to use drugs. He had gone to a Christian high school, so he knew all the right answers. The issue was repentance, and he didn't want to do that…Repenting means to make a turn, and that is what you see in the true Christian life.[4]

Did you catch the meaning of the word repentance? Mark described precisely why we use the moral law with our children. God's law teaches them that they are guilty sinners needing a new heart. God's Holy Spirit uses His law to teach us all we are guilty sinners deserving hell. God's saving grace opens our hearts to surrender our wills to Christ. The moral law points us to God through our sin so that He can create in each of us *a heart that hates evil*. As Proverbs 8:13 says, "The fear of the Lord is to hate evil."

What Happens If You Don't Train the Heart and Mind of a Child to Follow Jesus?

For the person that rejects Christ, the greatest consequence of his or her hardened and unrepentant heart will be the judgment and eternal wrath of God. Romans 2:5-8 warns:

> But in accordance with your hardness and your impenitent heart you are treasuring up for yourself wrath in the day of wrath and revelation of the righteous judgment of God, who "will render to each one according to his deeds": eternal life to those who by patient continuance in doing good seek for glory, honor, and immortality; but

to those who are self-seeking and do not obey the truth, but obey unrighteousness—indignation and wrath...

Studies show that, before they graduate from college, 70 to 88 percent of young people from *Christian* homes end up rejecting the faith they claimed to possess. When you consider the foundation of sand upon which worldviews are often built, it becomes evident why theirs collapses when secular winds and waves of skepticism, criticism, unbelief, and doubt undermine them.

Regrettably, the worldview of a typical Christian parent, Sunday School teacher, youth leader, and even pastor in America has been far too influenced by the thinking of the world. As a result, it is not really hard to understand why students graduate from our church youth groups and move on from Christian homes doctrinally illiterate, only to become easy prey for the enemy waiting to devour them. They have not truly opened their minds and hearts to sound doctrine. They have not repented of their sins and yielded to Christ.

Lest you think I'm sounding a false alarm, once again, numerous surveys document that the average self-professing Christian adult cannot explain—much less defend and pass on to his or her children—the essential Christian doctrines upon which a Biblical worldview are built. It stands to reason, then, that the teen in the average Christian home also cannot defend foundational Christian doctrines.

If we have not trained the hearts and minds of our children to love sound doctrinal teachings, then we should not be surprised that three-fourths of them eventually walk away from the faith in college. Unlike some of us, writers of Scripture were not in denial on this point. They warned that drifting from faith could happen:

> Beware lest anyone cheat you through philosophy and empty deceit, according to the tradition of men, according to the basic principles of the world, and not according to Christ. (Colossians 2:8)

One of the greatest rewards as a parent is watching your children live committed, godly lives and see them raise their children (your grandchildren!) to do the same. I urge you to commit now to rise above the world's standard of *good* parenting and make your goal *godly* parenting so Christ can be glorified in your life and family.

As I cautioned, training takes time, patience, sweat, hard work, and endurance, so whatever happens, *do not become discouraged*. We must love Christ and desire fervently that the hearts and minds of our children are set upon honoring Christ. We must want this so desperately that we understand every effort or struggle is more than worth it. The consequences are eternal. Sacrifice is never fun, but if you turn off that TV show or sporting event or forego that internet surfing session, and instead faithfully and prayerfully use and re-use this book and your Bible, you can prepare the hearts and minds of your children to follow Jesus Christ. Pray that by God's grace, they will.

BRANNON HOWSE
Founder & President, Worldview Weekends

INTRODUCTION

The overriding reason for you to read and talk through the questions in this book with your children is so they will develop hearts and minds for Christ. This is not some vague promise. You will see encouraging results in their lives. In fact, as I've lived and taught these training basics, I've identified 14 specific benefits to families and children, and I've detailed them below so you'll know what to expect.

1) By training our children in the foundational doctrines of sin, the accuracy of the Bible, and the death, burial and resurrection of Jesus Christ, we are preparing their hearts to seek God.

2) By training our children at an early age to recognize their sinfulness, we inculcate them with the understanding that sin has serious consequences and that doing God's will brings blessing.

3) When we don't address the sin natures of our children, we confront merely behavioral problems that are symptoms of their heart condition, not the root cause.

4) By training our children with Biblical doctrine at an early age and living it out before them, we show them the importance it plays in our home and life.

5) By training our children with the Scriptures at an early age, we are building into them a Christian worldview and preparing them to be thoroughly equipped for every good work, regardless of what vocation God may call them to (2 Timothy 3:16).

6) By training our children in Biblical doctrine, we are teaching them that God is sovereign—that He is in control and never caught by surprise. God's sovereignty gives us and our children hope, comfort, and peace in all circumstances, even when others are fearful, depressed, and defeated by the troubles of this world.

7) By training our children that we live according to the Bible because Scripture is a reflection of the character and nature of God, we encourage them to obey God's Word from hearts that desire a deeper relationship with their heavenly Father instead of fostering legalistic obedience.

8) When we train our children that God has placed them under the authority of their parents for protec-

tion and training in accordance with God's Word, we teach them to obey us from the heart so as to honor and obey God.

9) By training the heart of a child to obey God, we train our children to be pleasers of God, not of men. By contrast, if we teach our children to obey so they avoid punishment, a scolding, or to receive an award, we train them to jump through our hoops so they can keep us happy. Although a common approach, this does not train the heart but rather teaches them how to manipulate us and others. Training children with man-centered behavior modification only gives us the human equivalent of Pavlov's dogs rather than God-honoring young men and women. Note well: Children that are trained from the heart will seek to do the right thing even when we are not watching, because their motivation for doing right is not us but God.

10) By training our children in the essential doctrinal truths of Christianity, we prepare them to withstand the deception of false teachings and worldviews that will vie for their allegiance as they grow older. We are also equipping them with the knowledge they need to defend and contend for a Biblical worldview, as commanded of every Christian.

11) By training our children in a Biblical worldview, we grow in them Biblical values which produce Biblical conduct.

12) By developing in our children a love of Christian doctrine, we teach them to love knowledge and wisdom. Knowledge is the acquisition of truth, and wisdom is the application of truth.

13) By training our children in the ways of the Lord, we prepare each of them to seek a godly spouse and raise godly children, which produces a family that honors God and results in the blessing of a close-knit family.

14) By training our children in Christian doctrine, we not only develop their Biblical worldview, but we lay the foundation for a spiritual legacy that can reap benefits for generations to come and, ultimately, eternal rewards for those that come after us.

You see, there's a lot to look forward to, so let's get started.

1

WHAT IS A WORLDVIEW, AND WHY DOES IT MATTER?

When you look out the window, you don't usually think much about the glass you're looking through, do you? That's because a clear window simply allows you to see things outside the way they really are. Grass is green. Sky is blue. But suppose someone taped red plastic wrap all over the window. Things would suddenly look very different, wouldn't they? The grass might look brown or the sky purple. But that wouldn't be the real colors of those familiar things, would it? Of course not. Your ability to see colors accurately outside depends on whether or not your window is made of clear glass.

Something like that happens in the way people think about the world, too. How we understand what is around us is called our worldview. Whether or not people see things the way they really are depends entirely on their worldview.

Everything Starts with a Worldview

A worldview is the foundation of your values. Values determine how you act and how you live your life. Another way to describe a worldview is that it is a collection of your beliefs which make a difference in how you live.

Everyone has a worldview. You are surrounded by friends, other students, teachers, and even family members that have their own ways of looking at things. Some of them have views that are different from Christianity.

Various worldviews compete for the attention of your heart and mind, but unless a worldview lines up with the Bible (the clear glass through which we look at the world), it won't give you a real picture of how things are.

There are actually only three basic types of worldview. We call them Judeo-Christian (Jewish and Christian—like in the Old and New Testaments), Cosmic Humanism (also known as New Age thinking), and Secular Humanism.

What Different Worldviews Say about the Way Things Are

The Christian view on things begins with a belief in God. The Greek word for God is *theos*, so we call this a *theistic* worldview. Christians believe in the God described in the Bible.

A Cosmic Humanist believes in *pantheism*. That is the belief that everything—the world and all that is in it—is god. God is not a person, and, as a result, this version of god is not the God of the Bible. This "god" is a force you can use to your advantage through the power of your mind (kind of like "the force" in *Star Wars*).

The Secular Humanist worldview says there is no God at all. This is called atheism (*a*-theism means *not* theism). Therefore you can live your life as though you are God. A Secular Humanist does not believe in heaven or hell.

Christianity says there are both spiritual and natural worlds. A Cosmic Humanist believes only in the spiritual world and says the natural world is simply an illusion. The natural world doesn't really matter. At the other extreme, Secular Humanists believe in *naturalism*, which means they think all that exists is the natural world. There is no spiritual, or supernatural, side.

A Christian believes people need to be saved from their sins. That can happen only through repenting, believing in the death, burial, and resurrection of Jesus Christ, and accepting Him as Lord and Savior.

Cosmic Humanists believe people are saved through a process called reincarnation. They believe a person's soul passes repeatedly from one body to another until his or her good deeds (good karma) outweigh the bad deeds (bad karma). When that finally happens, the person becomes a spirit or master guide. They become part of the "Great Nothing."

A Secular Humanist believes that when people die, that's it. There is nothing beyond the grave.

Christians believe the world was created by God through His spoken word and that He is the source of all truth. People have a soul that will live forever in either heaven or hell, depending on whether or not they have repented and accepted Jesus Christ.

Since Cosmic Humanists believe the natural world is an illusion, it really doesn't matter to them how we got here. A Cosmic Humanist believes heaven and hell are merely a state of mind, or the way you choose to look at life.

A Secular Humanist believes in evolution, that the universe came about by chance. Cosmic and Secular Humanists both believe truth is relative, not a fixed absolute established by God. They believe people are basically good and do bad things only because of negative influences in the world. A Christian believes people are born with a sin nature but that each person does have a free will and can choose to be a slave to sin or a servant of Jesus Christ.

Basic Christian Ideas

Let's review what we have said about the three basic worldviews. Christian theism is centered on six main beliefs:

1. There is only one God;

2. The world was made by God;

3. People die and then are judged;

4. People can only be saved through acknowledging their sinfulness, repenting of their sins, and yielding their lives to Jesus Christ and the salvation He provides on the cross through His death, burial, and resurrection;

5. God is the source of all truth; and

6. There is a spiritual world and a natural world, and God created both.

Basic Ideas of Cosmic Humanism

Cosmic Humanism is also founded on six main beliefs:

1. God is not a personal God;

2. God is a force or energy field that you use to your advantage through the power of your mind;

3. God is everything and every thing is God—God is in the trees, the stars, the grass, animals, humans;

4. Life or the physical world is an illusion;

5. Man is not totally sinful but basically good;

6. Life promises everything and demands nothing; there are no rules so you can live however you want to (you're your own boss).

Basic Ideas of Secular Humanism

Secular Humanism is centered on the following five beliefs:

1. There is no God—therefore every person is his or her own god;

2. The only world that exists is what we see—there is no spiritual world;

3. There are no moral absolutes—people decide for themselves what is right or wrong;

4. The purpose of life is pleasure;

5. When you die, that is it, because there is no life after death.

As you read this book, you'll see how a worldview makes a difference in every part of your life. Everything matters to God. Therefore, everything is a religious issue. Even atheists—who hate God and His laws—have a religious worldview. Their belief about God is that He does not exist. But that's a strangely colored glass that seriously distorts their view of the world.

Pray This: Ask the Lord to sharpen your mind to think and live according to the Bible and a Christian worldview.

What Do You Think?

1. What is a worldview?

2. What are the three main worldviews?

3. How many of the main beliefs that make up a Christian worldview can you name?

4. How many of the main beliefs that make up a Cosmic Humanist worldview can you name?

5. How many of the main beliefs that make up a Secular Humanist worldview can you name?

2

GOD TELLS US ABOUT HIMSELF
THROUGH THE WORLD AROUND US

Have you ever thought that the house or apartment you live in just happened to fall together by accident?

Probably not. At least I hope not.

After all, when you look at a building or a house of any kind, you know it had a builder. It did not appear by chance, and it certainly didn't make itself.

What about a painting, did you ever stop to think did it just happen, or was there an artist who created it? When you see a painting, you know it was painted by a painter.

That is a natural way to think, of course. Someone designed and made the building you live in, the car you ride in, the chairs you sit on, and the books you read. So, when you look around and see people, birds, trees, stars, the moon, dogs, cats, and horses, you know they did not just happen all by themselves, either. Someone had to create them, and it makes perfect sense to think that the Someone is God.

As strange as it sounds, there are people who believe the universe and everything around us—from toads to people—were not created by God. They say it all just happened to appear out of nothing over a long period of time. A person who thinks the world happened by accident believes in what is called *evolution*. An evolutionist does not believe God created trees, flowers, horses, the moon, birds, or you.

As much as it makes sense to think Someone made what you see around you, we also have the Bible to explain where everything came from. It tells us in different places:

- Genesis 1:1, "In the beginning God created the heavens and the earth."

- Psalm 19:1, "The heavens declare the glory of God; And the firmament shows His handiwork."

Psalm 139:14 even talks specifically about you and me. King David, who wrote the psalm, tells God how amazed he is at how we are made: "I will praise You, for I am fearfully and wonderfully made."

You are one of the best examples anywhere of how well-designed our world is. I'll give you a sampling of the kind of things that are so marvelous, and I think you'll agree that Whoever made you was an Awesome Designer.

Be Mindful of Your Brain

Your brain weighs a little more than three pounds, but it can think in more ways than tons of computer equipment. That glob of stuff inside your head contains 15 billion "sensors" called *neurons*. They join together in more than 100 thousand billion (100,000,000,000,000!) connections. That's more than all the electrical connections in all the TVs, computers, DVD players, radios, and other electrical gadgets in the world!

Have a Heart!

Here's another amazing part of you: Your heart. It weighs less than a pound, but it is a little machine—a pump—that goes on working without any maintenance or oil changes for about 75 years.[5] Imagine having a car that would run that long without oil or repairs!

The Eyes Have It

And what about the body parts you're using to read this book? You've rolled your eyes before. Yet rolling is just the start of what they can do. Eyes can make more than 100,000 different motions, and when you step into a dark room, they can increase their ability to see the available light by 100,000 times. On top of that, your eyes come complete with automatic aiming, automatic focusing, and automatic maintenance while you sleep.[6]

Of *Course* There's a God, Right?

We've only looked at three of hundreds of your body parts, and yet it's easy to imagine that you were created by the all-powerful, all-knowing God of the universe. So why would someone *not* believe in God?

The answer is really very simple. People who don't believe in God simply don't *want* to. Someone that doesn't believe in God is called an *atheist*. Atheists do not want to read the Bible and live like God wants them to. They also prefer to believe in anything they feel like believing, whether it makes sense or not.

As I said, it makes more sense to believe God exists and that He made everything than to believe that He didn't and that everything "just happened." An atheist may say God doesn't exist, but that doesn't make it true. You could say the moon doesn't exist, but that wouldn't make the moon go away.

God wants everyone to believe He really is there. That's why He has created so many different things to reveal Himself in the world. He is the one true God and Creator of the universe.

Pray This: Thank God now for showing Himself through His creation to you, to me, and to everyone who will believe the sensible thing.

What Do You Think?

1. When you see a painting, you know it was created by whom?

2. People that believe everything was created by chance and not by God believe in what?

3. The reason evolutionists don't believe God created the universe is that they don't *want* to believe in Whom?

4. God wants every person to know Him, and so one way He reveals Himself is through what?

3

Truth Is a Who

Jesus once said, "I am the way, the truth, and the life" (John 14:6). It's such a meaningful statement that we could talk for a long time about every word in it, but I want to focus on the middle part, the word "truth."

You've been told many times to "tell the truth," and I hope you always do. What Jesus says here, though, sounds a little different than that, doesn't it? He says something special about Himself: *I am the truth*.

Truth Is a Person

It sounds as if we should be thinking that *Jesus is truth*, right? Jesus is God, so that means His character— who He is—is what makes truth.

Jesus is the truth we're supposed to share with the world. It is because of what we believe about life and death and eternity that we must share truth with as many people as we can.

The idea that truth is a person is what sets Christianity apart from all other religions. James 1:17-18 says, "Every good gift and every perfect gift is from above, and comes down from the Father of lights, with whom there is no variation or shadow of turning. Of His own will He brought us forth by the word of truth, that we might be a kind of firstfruits of His creatures." According to these verses, the Bible tells us all about the truth. The Bible explains the character and nature of God.

When Jesus says He is the way, the truth and the life, He means there is no way to receive salvation or reach heaven apart from Him. Practicing any other religion will be a waste of time. Many unbelievers are offended by Jesus' claim because it means their ideas of truth are wrong.

Christianity Is True Because Jesus Is Truth

Years ago, Josh McDowell set out to disprove Christianity but instead became one of the world's greatest defenders of Christianity and the Bible. Mr. McDowell talks about what it means that God is truth:

God is the original. He is the origin of all things that are in existence. And if we wish to know if anything is right or wrong, good or evil, we must measure it against the person who is true. "He is the Rock," Moses said, "His work is perfect...a God of truth and without iniquity, just and right is he" (Deuteronomy 32:4, KJV). You see, it is the very person and nature of God that defines truth. It is not something he measures up to. It is not something he announces. It is not even something he decides. It is something he is.[7]

Truth is a fixed standard for all time, people and places. It will always be wrong to steal, to lie or to commit murder. Why? Because, as we said before, truth is based on the character of God, and God does not change. Lying, stealing and murder go against the character and nature of God.

So there is a simple answer to the basic question of this chapter, "What is truth?" The answer: Truth is a person. Because God is truth, people who reject truth are rejecting God, whether they know it or not.

Ignoring Truth Won't Make It Go Away

Sadly, those who reject truth will have no excuse on Judgment Day. As 2 Thessalonians 2:10-11 says, "...they did not receive the love of the truth, that they might be saved. And for this reason God will send them strong delusion, that they should believe the lie." People who reject truth become stupid or purposeless. It is part of their punishment for rejecting God.

When people reject God over and over again they become so foolish that they do crazy things like worship idols, or statues made of wood or stone, or even animals (Romans 1:23). If a person doesn't worship God by serving and obeying Him, then whatever he or she does focus on becomes "god." Unfortunately, these people will end up in hell forever. You see, rejecting truth not only has consequences in this life but in the next life, too.

Pray This: Thank Jesus Christ right now for being the way, the truth, and the life. Thank Him that anyone who accepts Him as truth will get to go to heaven.

What Do You Think?

1. Who is the Way, the Truth and the Life?

2. What did God give us to read so we can learn more about the character and nature of God?

3. Other than "because the Bible says so," why is it wrong to steal, lie and murder?

4. Since God does not change, His character and nature will not change. What does that mean about truth?

5. When people reject truth, Whom are they really rejecting?

6. Since Jesus is the only Way, Truth and Life and no one comes to the Father except through Him, any religion that promises salvation apart from Jesus Christ is _____.

4

ARE ALL RELIGIONS EQUAL?

One of the most popular lies in the world today is that all religions are equally true. People will say strange things like, "Your beliefs may be true for you, but not for me." That's like saying, "The color black may be black to you, but it's white to me." Kind of silly, right?

So let's be sure to get one thing straight: It is a possibility that all religions are false, but *it is impossible for all of them to be true*.

Looking for the One Who Never Sinned

Dr. Erwin Lutzer is the pastor of a famous church in Chicago called the Moody Church. It has been around for more than 100 years. Dr. Lutzer also has been a speaker for my Worldview Weekends, and he has written many books about Christianity. He loves to tell people about Jesus and learn about what both Christians and non-Christians think about God. One time while doing that, he attended a huge meeting of people from all over the world. They had come to Chicago to talk about their religious beliefs.

Dr. Lutzer walked around the convention center where the meetings were being held and visited many of the people who were there (more than 7,000 people had come). He wrote a book about his talks with these people, and here is some of what he had to say:

> I walked through the display area in search of a sinless prophet/teacher/Savior. I asked a Hindu Swami whether any of their teachers claimed sinlessness. "No," he said, appearing irritated with my question, "If anyone claims he is sinless, he is not a Hindu!"
>
> What about Buddha? No, I was told, he didn't claim sinlessness.... He sought enlightenment and urged his followers to do the same. He died seeking enlightenment. No sinlessness here....
>
> When I came to the representatives of the Muslim faith, I already knew that in the Koran the prophet Mohammed admitted he was in need of forgiveness. They agreed. "There is one God, Allah, and Mohammed was not perfect." Again, no sinlessness there.

Why was I searching for a sinless Savior?...
Since I'm a sinner, I need someone who is standing on higher ground.

Understandably, none of the religious leaders I spoke with even claimed to have a Savior. Their prophets, they said, showed the way, but made no pretense to be able to personally forgive sins or transform so much as a single human being. Like a street sign, they gave directions, but were not able to take us where we need to go. If we need any saving, we will have to do it ourselves.

The reason is obvious: No matter how wise, no matter how gifted, no matter how influential other prophets, gurus, and teachers might be, they had the presence of mind to know that they were imperfect just like the rest of us....

What did Jesus have to say about His sinless life?

"Which of you convicts Me of sin? If I speak truth, why do you not believe Me?" (John 8:46).

Pilate, who longed to find fault with Christ, confessed, "I find no fault in this Man" (Luke 23:4).

Peter, who lived with Him for three years, said he "committed no sin, nor was deceit found in His mouth" (1 Peter 2:22).

As C. E. Jefferson put it, "The best reason we have for believing in the sinlessness of Jesus is the fact that He allowed His dearest friends to think that He was."[8]

No One Else Has It

All the religious leaders who have ever lived—such as Buddha, Confucius, and Mohammad—have the same thing in common. They all sinned, and they are all dead. In fact, Buddha admitted that he wasn't even sure if God exists, and he spent his whole life searching for truth. Buddha sure couldn't have been the savior of the world if he was still trying to figure out what the truth is! Jesus Christ didn't have to search for truth because He Himself is truth (you'll remember we talked about that in Chapter 3).

Millions of Muslims believe Mohammad was a special prophet of God. He wrote a book called the Koran, and in the Koran Mohammad confessed that he was in need of forgiveness. What kind of savior says he needs someone to forgive him? How could Mohammad save the world if he could not save himself? He couldn't, of course.

The One and Only

Jesus not only claimed to be sinless, but He claimed to be able to forgive the sins of others. That's because He was and is the world's only sinless Savior. Jesus even challenged the people that hated Him to point out one sin that He had committed, but guess what? Not even Jesus' enemies could name a single thing He had done wrong. Wow! Even people who opposed Jesus could not name a sin they had ever seen Him commit!

What sets Jesus Christ apart from all the religious leaders of the world is that He was the sinless Savior, and He is still alive. All religions and worldviews that go against that truth are lies. These lies come from Satan, who the Bible says is the father of lies.

Remember I admitted at the beginning of this chapter that all religions could be false, but they cannot all be true? Only one religion can be true, and that one is Christianity. Christianity is true because Jesus Christ is the risen, sinless Savior.

Pray This: Thank God that He has given you the chance to know Jesus and to believe in Christianity, the only true religion. Ask the Lord to help you tell other people about the truth of Jesus Christ whenever you have the chance.

What Do You Think?

1. All religions can be wrong, but they cannot all be

   _____.

2. Every religious leader who ever lived, except Jesus Christ, died and is still dead—True or false?

3. Buddha, Mohammed and other religious leaders spent their lives searching for truth. Why didn't Jesus Christ have to search for truth?

4. If a religious leader claims to be able to save you, he must first be able to save whom?

5. Christianity is truth because Jesus Christ is sinless and did what after He died on the cross?

5

How Do We Know
the Bible Is True?

The Bible is a remarkable book. There is literally none other like it. It was written over a period of 1,400 years (14 centuries!). On top of that, there were more than 40 different authors from three continents (Africa, Asia, and Europe), who wrote in three different languages.

Even though this background could have produced a very confusing book, the Bible tells a consistent story from beginning to end. And—get this—it is without error. It can be trusted to tell the truth about God all the way from the first book (Genesis) through hundreds of pages to Revelation (the last book).

Why? Because the authors wrote the Bible as they were led by God.

Just Ask the Bible to Know What's Ahead

One way we know the Bible can be trusted is that it is full of what we call "predictive prophecy." Predictive prophecy occurs when the Bible tells about things that are going to happen years in advance of when the events actually occur, and then the whole prediction comes true! Scripture records many, many prophecies that came about just as the Bible said they would.

One example is the nation of Israel. The Bible predicted Israel would become a nation again after centuries of the Jewish people having no place for their own country. Israel had not been a nation for more than 2,000 years, but in 1948, it became a nation just as the Word of God had predicted in the Old Testament:

• Ezekiel 45:12 even tells what kind of money would be used in the new Israel. Modern Jewish money is called the shekel.

• Ezekiel 37:21 explains that the Jewish people would return to Israel from all over the world— just as they have.

• Zephaniah 3:9 foretells that the official language of Israel will be Hebrew, and today, newspapers in Israel are printed in Hebrew.

• Ezekiel 36:26–35 and Isaiah 27:6 prophesy that the desert of Israel will become like a garden. Can you imagine growing fruit, flowers and vegetables in the desert? God foretold this would happen, and today an Israeli farmer, working desert land, produces four to six times as much food as an average farmer in America. Israel actually sends large amounts of fruit and flowers to other countries—all from a desert!

• Ezekiel 37:10 says the nation of Israel will have a great army. During the last 50 years, Israel's army, air force, and intelligence agency have proven to be among the best trained and most powerful in the world.

The Know-It-All Book

The Bible also makes predictions about things other than Israel. For instance, Daniel 12:4 says technology will produce a huge increase in knowledge, speed of transportation, and worldwide communications. Consider these examples of progress:

• Has there been an increase in knowledge? You bet there has! Experts estimate that in the last 50 years, there has been more scientific progress than in the previous 5,000 years!

• Do we travel at high rates of speed? Yes! Before 1830, people traveled only by horse, foot, or sailboat. From 1830 to 1890, we invented steam engines, which gave us trains and ships. From 1890 to today, people have developed cars and jets, as well as spacecraft capable of traveling to the moon. We have even landed unmanned spacecrafts on the planet Mars.

• Are there worldwide communications? You see examples of this every day. On television, you can watch live events that are taking place on the other side of the earth, and you can talk on the phone or e-mail people that live thousands of miles away.

The Bible made all these predictions accurately because it is a supernatural book that was written by a supernatural God.

Dig This: Archeology Tells the Same Story

Another way we know that what we read in the Bible is true is through archeology. Archeology is the study of ancient cities and people. Researchers dig for buried pots, art, buildings, tombs, and other remains from ancient life.

Archeologists have made more than 25,000 discoveries related to the Old Testament and found just what the Bible talks about in every case. These scientists have uncovered proof that the kings mentioned in the Bible actually existed and that the cities described were real.

The Right Book to Believe In

Some people claim the Bible isn't accurate because it has been copied so many times by different people. But between 1947 and 1956, handwritten copies of every book of the Old Testament except one were found in caves in Israel. These copies are known as the Dead Sea Scrolls because they were found near the Dead Sea, and they're about 2,000 years old.

What makes the Dead Sea Scrolls so important is that these copies of Bible books say the same thing we read in our Bibles today. Nothing has been changed even after 20 centuries of making copies!

This way of knowing the Bible is true also works for the New Testament as well as the Old Testament. Scholars have thousands of old copies called manuscripts. A manuscript is a handwritten copy of the original or a handwritten copy of another copy. Although there are no original versions of New Testament books (an original is called an "autograph"), there are more manuscripts of the New

Testament than of any other book ever written—24,286, to be exact. Like the Dead Sea Scrolls, these copies prove that the Bible of today is just as it was originally written 2,000 years ago.

So one thing is clear: there is plenty of proof that the Bible is true, accurate, and can be trusted!

Pray This: Thank God right now for protecting and preserving His Word so we will know how much God loves us, how He wants us to live, and how we can be saved from our sins by trusting in His Son, Jesus Christ. Thank the Lord that His Word is trustworthy.

What Do You Think?

1. Who told the men that wrote the Bible what to write?

2. What is it called when the Bible predicts an event and it comes true?

3. Not a single predictive prophecy contained in the Bible has ever been what?

4. The 100% accuracy of the Bible is a reason we think it is a _____ book.

5. Archeologists used to try dig to disprove the Bible, but they discovered everything it says is true. So now what do they read to find out where they should dig?

6. There are more manuscripts of the New Testament than what other book(s)?

6

ADAM AND EVE AND THE RESULTS OF THEIR SIN

Some people complain that so many bad things happen in the world that God must not care. In fact, many people use the bad things as an excuse not to believe in God at all.

It's true that there is much bad (evil) in the world, but people who blame it on God have it backwards. None of the bad is God's fault. Even though most of us don't like to admit it, the evil in the world is *our* fault. *People* do the bad things, and it's been going on for a long time. It started with the first two people God ever made. You've probably heard of them: Adam and Eve.

To see why evil is really our fault, you have to pay attention to how God meant for things to be in the first place. Then see what happened when Adam and Eve goofed it up. Let me explain.

God's Great Plan

God could have created the entire universe in just an instant. Instead, He chose to make everything in six days and then take a rest on the seventh day. God did this so we would follow His example of working six days and resting on the seventh. On the seventh day, called the Sabbath, we are to put all our work aside and spend the entire day resting and worshipping the God of the universe. The day of rest is one part of the big plan God started when He made the world.

The Creation Plan

On the first day of creation, God made the most basic part of our everyday life. He made light and darkness—day and night. You may not have thought of that before, but back when there was nothing, day and night didn't exist. You have to admit God made a pretty good system when He thought that one up.

On the second day, God created the sky and water and put them in separate places. Sky was "up." Water was "down."

On the third day, God created land and sea and all the plants. That's when He made oceans, mountains, flowers, vegetables, fruits, and trees.

On the fourth day, God created the sun, moon, and stars. He had already created day and night but made the sun, moon, and stars to be the "managers" of day and night.

On the fifth day, God created fish and other animals that live in water. He also made birds.

On the sixth day, God created cows, horses, snakes, lizards, lions, bears, dogs, and all other animals that live on land. On that same day, God took some dirt and formed a man. He breathed into the man's nose, and he became a living soul. God called him Adam.

After that, God pointed out that it was not good for the man to be by himself. He needed other people to be friends with and to have a family. So God put Adam to sleep, and He operated on him. God took out one of Adam's ribs and formed it into another person. But this person wasn't exactly like Adam. It was a woman whom Adam later named Eve.

God's Plan for a Perfect World

God made Adam and Eve married to each other and gave them a beautiful place to live called the Garden of Eden. They could eat whatever fruit they wanted from any tree except one. He specifically commanded Adam and Eve not to eat from a tree called the Tree of the Knowledge of Good and Evil. God warned the man and woman that if they ate from that tree, they would die.

The garden was a perfect place because it was like heaven on earth. Adam and Eve did not have to work for their food. When they got hungry they simply picked fruit from the trees. They also got along great with God back in those days. Every evening, God would call for Adam and Eve, and they would walk and talk together. Life was perfect.

The Big-Time Mess-Up

One day Eve ran into Satan, who had gotten into the garden and made himself into the form of a snake. He struck up a conversation with Eve as he slithered on the branches of the Tree of the Knowledge of Good and Evil. Satan suggested to Eve that she might like to eat the fruit from the tree, but Eve told him God had said she and Adam were not to do that. She said they weren't even supposed to touch it, or they would die.

Then Satan lied to Eve. He told her she wouldn't really die if she ate the fruit, and he tried to make God look bad. "What God doesn't want you to know," he said, "is that when you eat the fruit from this tree, you will become like Him. You'll know everything and be able to decide for yourself what is right and what is wrong. God just doesn't want you to be as smart as He is."

Now Eve liked the idea of being as smart as God (of course, she wouldn't really be that smart—Satan was lying, remember?—but she wanted to believe the serpent). Not only that, the fruit looked delicious. So Eve took fruit from the Tree of the Knowledge of Good and Evil, and she ate it. Even worse, she gave some of it to her husband, Adam. And still worse, he decided to do what his wife wanted instead of God (they teamed up against God), and he ate the forbidden fruit, too. What a bad scene!

The Results of Messing Up Perfection

Not long after Adam and Eve ate the fruit they weren't supposed to, God called them for their nightly walk, but they were hiding from Him. He knew what had happened but asked why they were hiding. They said they were embarrassed because they were not wearing clothes. Strange, that had never bothered them before. So God asked Adam and Eve who told them they were naked. He also asked them, point blank, if they had eaten fruit from the tree that He had commanded them not to.

Knowing they had been caught, Adam and Eve confessed that they had believed the lies of Satan and had disobeyed. They had committed the first sin (sin is anything you do that God doesn't want you to).

Adam and Eve now had to suffer the consequences of their sin, and, just as God had said, they died spiritually (later they would die physically). They were torn away from living a happy life with God because they decided to do things their own way. That's when the badness in the world got started.

One of the results that happened right away was that God made them leave the Garden of Eden. He even placed an angel armed with a flaming sword at the gateway to the garden so they could never enter again.

Because Adam and Eve disobeyed God, sin entered into the world. With it came death, disease, suffering, and all sorts of evil. God had planned to provide everything they needed, but because Adam and Eve decided they didn't want God around, they were forced to work hard to have food to eat, shelter, and clothes.

Adam and Eve's sin caused them to miss out on God's very best. They could no longer walk and talk with God in the happiness of the garden.

God Sets Things Right Again

Because of what Adam and Eve did, every person born after them has also been sinful. All people have been destined to die and be punished forever. Thankfully, though, that's not the way God wanted to leave things.

He loved people so much that He sent His Son Jesus Christ to be a sacrifice for us on the cross. Therefore, anyone who confesses their sins and follows Jesus will be saved. They will be guaranteed to spend eternity in heaven where we can be in God's presence once again.

Pray This: Thank God for sending His Son, Jesus Christ, to be the sinless sacrifice for your sins.

What Do You Think?

1.   God created the world in how many days?

2.   True or false: God commanded that Adam and Eve not eat the fruit from the Tree of Knowledge of Good and Evil.

3.   Name one lie Satan told Adam and Eve when he took the form of a serpent and encouraged them to eat the forbidden fruit.

4.   What was the consequence of Adam's and Eve's sin?

5.   Because of the sin that entered into the world through Adam and Eve, God had to send His only Son Jesus Christ to do what?

7

The Reason to Be Glad
You Sometimes Feel Guilty

Have you ever done something wrong and felt really guilty about it? I know you have.

How do I know?

Because every single person—both children and grown-ups—have felt guilty about something, some time. All people have a "signal" inside that tells them right from wrong. That signal is called a conscience.

Even though every person has *felt* his or her conscience, there's something about a conscience that very few people have ever *thought about*: Where did my conscience come from? Everybody just accepts that it's there, but the fact is, a conscience had to get started somehow. In fact, when you think about that conscience question, it tells you a lot about God.

The Image Thing

Right at the beginning of the Bible, in the book of

Genesis, we find out that all people are created in the "image" of God (Genesis 1:26). God is perfect (the Bible calls Him holy) because He wants and does only what is loving and right. God gives us our example of right and wrong. So a big part of being in God's image is that each person has a sense of right and wrong programmed into his or her mind and heart. That's what a conscience is.

This right and wrong has been called "the moral law" because it is how we know what good morals are. The moral law reflects God's character or nature. Everything that goes along with the nature of God is true and good, and everything against the character of God is false or bad.

The reason we know we shouldn't murder other human beings is that murder goes against the nature of God. It's not what He wants. We're not supposed to lie, steal, or break any of the other Ten Commandments because doing those things would also go against the character of God.

Ignoring It Won't Make the Sin Go Away

So why don't people always follow their consciences? Romans 2:15 says people "show the work of the law written in their hearts, their conscience also bearing witness, and between themselves their thoughts accusing or else excusing them." This verse means that people can either accept the guilty feeling that comes with breaking the law, or they can ignore it. If they ignore the guilt often enough, their consciences will become "seared" (1 Timothy 4:2). They'll get to the point where they don't even know the difference between right and wrong.

Although God has "written" the law in the conscience of every person, not everyone believes in God. Yet it doesn't make much sense to think there can be a conscience without God. As I said, it had to come from somewhere, and the most sensible idea is that there is a holy and righteous God who will also judge the world according to the moral law He's told us.

Built-in Knowledge

The word "conscience," by the way, has a very significant meaning. "Con" means "with," and "science" means "knowledge." Everyone is "with knowledge" of right and wrong. No one has any excuse for doing evil. When we sin against God, we do it knowing that it is sin. This includes everyone, whether Christian or not. One of the reasons God put the moral law in us is so we will know God exists.

We can ignore or deny God, but because He has made Himself known by creating us in His image and by placing knowledge of His character in our hearts, no one will have an excuse at judgment for rejecting God. Romans 1:20 says people "are without excuse."

No one can claim to deserve heaven because he or she has "lived a good enough life." God's standard is the moral law, and no one has kept the law perfectly. Romans 3:20 says no one "will be justified in His sight" by the "deeds of the law" because no one has obeyed everything in the moral law. Romans 3:10 says this loud and clear: "There is none righteous, no, not one," and Romans 3:23 concludes that "all have sinned and fall short of the glory of God."

Turn Away!

The law makes us aware of our sins. Everyone but Jesus Christ has broken the law. Anyone who has not repented of his or her sins and trusted in the death, burial, and resurrection of Jesus will not be pardoned for breaking the moral law. To repent means to stop doing the same bad things over and over. This does not mean you will never again sin, but there is a big difference between stumbling into sin and diving in on purpose.

The Bible talks a lot about repentance. Unless someone repents, there is no forgiveness of sins and therefore no salvation. John the Baptist preached in the wilderness, "Repent, for the kingdom of heaven is at hand!" (Matthew 3:2). Jesus sent out His twelve disciples two by two and told them to go out and preach "that people should repent" (Mark 6:12). Even Jesus spread the same message. Mark 1:14-15 says, "...Jesus came to Galilee, preaching the gospel of the kingdom of God, and saying, 'The time is fulfilled, and the kingdom of God is at hand. Repent, and believe in the gospel.'"

The moral law is the standard by which God will judge the world. Since every person has broken the moral law, unless people admit their sins and repent, they will not be saved. So pay attention to your conscience!

Pray This: Thank the Lord for placing the moral law in your heart so you can know what is consistent with the character and nature of God. Also thank the Lord that even though we have broken the moral law, He is willing to forgive us. Pray that the moral law will remind unbelievers that they have rebelled against God, and pray that they will confess their sins, repent, and live as God wants them to.

What Do You Think?

1. Who created your conscience?

2. What does your conscience do?

3. What does "conscience" mean?

4. The moral law, or the Ten Commandments, is God's standard and a reflection of His character and nature. The moral law shows us that we are what?

5. Why can no one claim he or she is going to heaven because of being "a good person"?

6. The reason people are permitted into heaven is not that they are good, but only if they what?

8

It's True: The Man Jesus Christ Is Also God

No one who really knows history will deny that Jesus Christ was a real man who lived about 2,000 years ago. Jesus was not a myth, and everyone knows it (a "myth," by the way, is a popular story that is not true). Some people say it *is* a myth, though, that Jesus is God, but that's not a myth, either. There are good reasons why we know this.

A Lifeguard That Can't Swim?

All of Christianity is based on believing that Jesus is God. So knowing whether or not He really is becomes very important.

Only God could be a perfect Savior. Someone who is just a man would do things wrong, and a sinful savior would be like a lifeguard that can't swim. How could a lifeguard save someone who is drowning if he or she couldn't even swim out to get the person? A lifeguard like that would be useless.

The same is true with a Savior that sins. The way God set things up, only a perfect savior can save sinful people.

So how do we know Jesus is God? Someone who claims to be God could surely prove He *is* God, right? Jesus Himself gave more than enough signs to show Who He is. On top of that, the whole Bible points to Him as someone extremely special.

Scripture Says, "I Told You So"

Even before Jesus was born, the Old Testament was hard at work telling everyone what the Son of God would be like. God wanted people to know what to look for so there would be no mistaking the Savior when He showed up.

The Bible contains 109 specific prophecies the Messiah would fulfill (the word "Messiah" is another name given to Jesus). These predictions describe the life, ministry, death, burial, and rising from the dead of Jesus Christ. They were written centuries before Jesus was born, and Jesus fulfilled every single one of the prophecies about the Messiah.

Dr. Norman Geisler is an expert on the life of Jesus, and he points out a few of these prophecies:

1. The Christ (Messiah) will be born of a woman (Genesis 3:15).

2. He will be born of a virgin (Isaiah 7:14).

3. He will be of the seed of Abraham (Genesis 12:1–3; 22:18).

4. He will be of the tribe of Judah (Genesis 49:10; Luke 3:23, 33).

5. He will be of the House of David (2 Samuel 7:12; Matthew 1:1).

6. His birthplace will be Bethlehem (Micah 5:2; Matthew 2:1).

7. He will be anointed by the Holy Spirit (Isaiah 11:2; Matthew 3:16–17).

8. He will be heralded by a messenger of God (Isaiah 40:3; Matthew 3:1–2).

9. He will perform miracles (Isaiah 35:5–6; Matthew 9:35).

10. He will cleanse the temple (Malachi 3:1; Matthew 21:12).

11. He will be rejected by His own people (Psalm 118:22; 1 Peter 2:7).

12. He will die some 483 years after 444 B.C. (Daniel 9:24).

13. He will die a humiliating death (Psalm 22; Isaiah 53; Matthew 27.

14. He will rise from the dead (Psalm 16:10; Mark 16:6; Acts 2:31).

15. He will ascend into heaven (Psalm 68:18; Acts 1:9).

16. He will sit at the right hand of God (Psalm 110:1; Hebrews 1:3).[9]

"Faking It" Didn't Make It

A man named Tim LaHaye has studied Bible prophecy for years and says the possibility that even as few as "20 of these 109 prophecies could be fulfilled in one man by chance is less than one in one quadrillion, one hundred and twenty-five trillion. Most people cannot even imagine such a number. If they did, it would look something like this: 1 in 1,125,000,000,000,000."[10] That's a big number, and it means Jesus has to be the one the prophecies were talking about.

People who don't believe the message of the Bible often say the prophecies were really written after Jesus lived. They say the people who wrote them down were trying to fake us out—to make us believe in Jesus when He really wasn't special at all.

But don't believe anyone who tries to tell you that. It is a fact of history that large portions of the Old Testament (which contains these 109 prophecies) were written long before the birth of Jesus Christ. Again, no real expert will deny that. Our friend Dr. Geisler says, "Even the most liberal critic of the Old Testament admits to the completion of the prophetic books by some four hundred years before Christ and the book of Daniel by about 165 B.C."[11] (B.C. means Before Christ, or before the birth of Christ.)

Miracles Tell the Real Story

Another reason we know Jesus is God is His miracles. He did some amazing things like changing water into wine, healing blind people, and making crippled people be able to walk. He even brought two different people back to life after they had died.

One proof that Jesus performed these miracles is that even His enemies admitted He did them. Since the ones who doubted Jesus did not want to say He was the Messiah, they claimed Jesus did miracles by the power of Satan. You see, they didn't deny the miracles, just the source. But it doesn't make much sense to think the devil would do so many good things for people, does it? The reasonable explanation is that our loving God did them.

The evidence shows that Jesus Christ was and is God. You know what that means? It means Jesus can save us from our sins because He is God and lived a sinless life. He made it so that we can live forever with Him.

Pray This: Thank Jesus Christ right now for coming to earth as a man and as God and for being our sinless Savior. Thank Him for dying on the cross so we can turn from our sins and be saved.

What Do You Think?

1. A Savior that sins would be like a lifeguard that cannot _____.

2. The Bible gives lots of evidence that Jesus Christ was and is God. For instance, how many specific prophecies did Jesus Christ fulfill?

3. The mathematical probability that one person could fulfill all 109 specific prophecies about Jesus is so unlikely that the fact that Jesus Christ fulfilled them proves He is what?

4. True or false: It is an historical fact that the 109 prophecies concerning Jesus Christ were written before the birth of Jesus Christ.

5. Even the critics of Jesus Christ did not deny that He performed miracles, but they said He did them by the power of what?

9

You're "Okay"
Only Because of Jesus

"Love…your neighbor as yourself."

When Jesus said that in Luke 10:27, He was actually quoting Leviticus 19:18 in the Old Testament. So the idea had been around for centuries even before Jesus came to earth.

Since you're to love others "as yourself," it seems like Jesus is saying you can't love others without loving yourself, right? But true followers of Jesus Christ should not love themselves as the world describes love.

Selfish Esteem

A lot of people like to talk about "self-esteem." That's not the same thing as Biblical self-love, though. In the verses Jesus uses from Leviticus, God explains that we should treat others respectfully in our daily lives. We should do things for them that we would also do to take care of ourselves. It *doesn't* mean we're supposed to think of ourselves as being worthy of love because we're so good.

Jesus wants us to do what is good for others and not just think of our own well-being. "Thinking only of yourself" might be the natural thing for most people, but many times, it is also the sinful thing. Jesus says not to be selfish or self-centered.

Take Care of Yourself!

The good, Biblical self-love refers to a person's natural desire to watch out for his or her own welfare. This can be simply a matter of survival. Our instincts tell us to try to stay alive. They also make us want to do things that are pleasurable, not painful. That's why you eat when you're hungry and sleep when you're tired. This kind of self-love makes you look both ways before crossing the street, to brush your teeth so they don't rot (you do that every night, right?), to wear a helmet when riding your bike (yes?), or to get out of the pool when you hear thunder so you don't get struck by lightning. It is an automatic reaction that gives human beings enough sense to "get in out of the rain."[12]

Biblical self-love is common to all people—Christians as well as non-Christians. It is natural and effortless. You don't have to take lessons to learn to do it. However, this thing called self-esteem is very different.

What's Bad about Thinking You're Good

Self-esteem is a way of saying people are basically good and that they are not completely in need of Jesus Christ and His sacrifice on the cross. It implies that we are good enough to face judgment on our own and that all the cross did was to help us out a little bit. The Bible, however, tells us not to "boast except in the cross of our Lord Jesus Christ" (Galatians 6:14).

None of us are good, honorable, or deserving of respect based on who we are. The Bible says there is no one good "no, not one" (Romans 3:23). Believing in Christ is what gives our lives merit. The only way to be worthy of reward is when a person dies to himself or herself (read Romans 6 and 8 to see what this is all about). The Bible says that apart from Christ we can do nothing, for we are like filthy rags or a little worm.

Dying for the Chance to Live

Sometimes "dying to self" means giving up even the self-preservation kind of love we said is okay. Christians that have surrendered their lives to Christ may be called to places that are not safe, secure, comfortable, or free of danger.

If the martyrs of Christian history (we talk about some of them in Chapter 11) had put the instinct of self-love before their Christian calling, they would not have let anyone kill them for their beliefs. But by preaching the gospel when it was against the law, torture and death were often what happened. The martyrs denied the basic reflex of self-love because they placed a higher priority on fulfilling the will of God through their lives.

In today's world where many people think self-worship is all right, Christians must reject the false version of self-love. We also must be willing to reject the natural impulse for comfort and self-preservation when it conflicts with God's desire for us to live the way the Bible tells us to. That may not always make us feel good on the outside, but it is the way Jesus said we would live an "abundant life" with the kind of good things He will give us.

Pray This: Since we are sinful, thank God that He has given us Jesus to make us able to receive salvation, because otherwise there would be no way to get to heaven. Ask Him to help you love others as you love yourself, the Biblical way.

What Do You Think?

1. The Bible tells us that we must boast (brag) only about what?

2. The self-love Jesus was talking about in Luke 10:27 was not a self-centered, selfish love, but a self-love that causes us to do such daily activities as what?

3. As Christians, our worth is not found in ourselves but in what Jesus Christ can do through us. Only believing in Christ gives our lives _____.

10

How We Know Jesus Christ Came Back to Life

Since the Bible tells the story very clearly about Jesus coming back to life after He died, you may never have thought about the possibility that some people don't think the story is true. They assume that when people die, they're dead, and that's that. Jesus is different than anyone else who ever lived, of course, so we know He certainly could—and did—rise from the dead. The people who doubt that just don't know the facts.

The resurrection of Jesus is one of the most for-sure events in all of history. Even so, you might think it's fun to know the strange and silly-sounding explanations doubters have for the disappearance of Jesus' body after He was crucified.

Oops—Wrong Tomb!

Some people try to explain away the resurrection by saying the disciples went to the wrong tomb to see the body of Jesus. Don't you just hate it when that happens? But really: How could it be the wrong tomb if the women and the disciples found the clothes there that Jesus had been buried in?

Oh, and do you suppose the Roman soldiers also forgot where the tomb was? The grave was closed with a Roman seal that had to be broken in order to open it back up. If the disciples had gone to the wrong tomb, the Jewish authorities and the Romans could have stopped the resurrection story simply by pointing the women and the disciples to the correct tomb. There they would have found the Roman seal and the still-dead body of Jesus. But no one ever found Jesus in another grave somewhere.

And consider this: The tomb that was used for the body of Jesus had been provided by a rich man named Joseph of Arimathea. The Bible says the tomb was brand new. Do you think Joseph, after spending lots and lots of money to have someone carve out a small cave in stone, would forget where it was? I wouldn't have if it were my money!

Grave Robbers!

"But," a few doubters suggest, "Maybe someone stole the body."

Now there's an idea!

Some claim the disciples stole the body to make it look like Jesus had risen from the dead. That raises some pretty hard questions, though:

1. How could the disciples have moved a stone away from the tomb without waking up the guards (assuming they were sleeping—which they probably weren't, since guards could be executed for falling asleep while on duty)?

2. Disturbing a tomb could get you the death penalty, so do you really think the disciples would risk being killed for raiding the tomb just to pull off a fake resurrection? Remember, the disciples were a very unhappy group of people after Jesus was crucified. Since they hadn't expected Jesus to come back to life, they were probably too scared to pull off anything like stealing His body.

3. Even if the disciples had wanted to steal Jesus' body, and if they could have gotten by the guards, how would they have moved the stone that blocked the tomb? Josh McDowell is a man who has studied a lot about the history of Jesus' life and death. He found out that an early copy of the Bible says the stone was so big that not even

20 men together could move it![13] The Bible says the stone was moved by an angel from heaven, not by the disciples or the women.

4. If the Jewish or Roman leaders really believed the disciples had stolen the body of Jesus, why didn't they have the disciples killed for disturbing a grave? If the body of Jesus was still in the tomb and the disciples were lying about the resurrection, the authorities would have put the body on display to put an end to the story. Or if the rulers had taken the body of Jesus to a secret location, they could have brought it out for everyone to see.

5. If the body of Jesus was stolen, why were the grave clothes still in the tomb, folded neatly, just as you would expect if Jesus had slipped out of them supernaturally? They wouldn't be.

Since it's so easy to show that Jesus' body was not stolen or moved by someone, there are other doubters who say Jesus wasn't really dead when He was put in the tomb.

Yeah, right.

It sounds pretty stupid to say that, and so do some of

the explanations about how He managed to stay alive.

Maybe He Just Fainted

Some people say Jesus didn't die. He just passed out on the cross. This is called the swoon theory ("swoon" is another word for "faint"). Supposedly, Jesus simply passed out, was taken down from the cross, and the cool air in the tomb revived Him.

Roman executioners were way too good at their job, though, to let something like that happen. Sometimes, just to make sure the person on the cross was dead, the guards would break the legs so the victim could not push himself up to breathe. That way, the condemned person would finally die from suffocation. It's pretty horrible, but that's what they did.

When the guards came to break Jesus' legs, He was already dead. To make sure, one soldier stabbed his spear into Jesus' side. Blood and water poured out. If Jesus were not dead when the soldier jabbed Him, only blood would have come out. Both blood and water come out only if the person is dead.

Doctors who have studied the Bible agree that Jesus was dead when taken down from the cross. Not only that, but there was a rule among the Romans that they would not take someone down from a cross until six soldiers agreed that the person was dead.

Besides, even if Jesus had simply fainted and was re-vived by the cool air in the tomb, how could He have moved away the stone that would have taken more than 20 healthy men to put in place? Not gonna happen.

Add to that what Jesus would have looked like to His disciples if He had made it out. The disciples may have been glad to see Him, but they sure wouldn't have been very inspired by a half-dead man. That's not much to preach about.

You're Seeing Things

The hallucination theory is the belief that everyone who reported seeing Jesus was "seeing things." According to the Bible, there were more than 500 people who saw Jesus after He had died. Doctors say that large groups of people never imagine seeing the same thing at the same time. One person may dream up something crazy, but it doesn't happen to whole groups. Besides, Jesus appeared to the disciples many times during a 40-day period. He even ate meals with them. No one's ever heard of a hal-lucination sitting down for dinner.

After Jesus ascended into heaven (while His disciples watched), none of them said they saw Jesus again. So in order to accept the hallucination theory, someone would have to believe that the hallucinations of the disciples were all the same and that they started and stopped at the same time.

I don't think so.

The Eyewitnesses Have It

As I said earlier, more than 500 people saw Jesus at one time. But in addition to Jesus' friends, He also appeared to one of the greatest enemies of Christianity, Saul of Tarsus.

Saul was a Jewish leader who killed many Christians. The first one was Stephen, and you can read the story of his death in Acts 7:54-60. Yet, when Jesus Christ appeared to Saul, he was completely changed and became one of the greatest preachers of Christianity. In Acts 26, by the way, Saul (who became known as Paul after meeting Jesus) gives his testimony. What would change such a man from hating, persecuting, and killing Christians to becoming a strong defender of Christianity? The most likely explanation is exactly what Paul said it was: He saw Jesus and talked to Him.

It's so obvious that the Bible's stories about Jesus rising from the dead are true that it's hard to imagine why people bother trying to make up reasons it didn't happen. But here's why they do: They just don't want to accept the truth because it would mean they'd have to live their lives God's way instead of their own way.

Pray This: Thank the Lord Jesus that the Bible does such a good job of telling what happened after Jesus died and came back to life. Also thank Him that He helped you know it's true. Ask the Lord Jesus to help you be a stronger follower of Him, like His disciples.

What Do You Think?

1. How do we know that on resurrection day the disciples and women did not go to the wrong tomb?

2. How do we know the disciples did not steal the body of Jesus in order to make it look like He had risen from the dead?

3. What did Jesus leave in the tomb to show that the disciples were at the right place?

4. How do we know Jesus did not just pass out on the cross?

5. How many healthy men would it have taken to roll away the stone from the tomb?

6. After His resurrection, Jesus met with the disciples many times over a 40-day period. He walked, talked, and even ate meals with the disciples. How big was one of the crowds Jesus appeared to after He arose?

11

WOULD YOU DIE FOR A LIE?

Frank Harber is now the pastor of a large church in Texas, but, years ago, he was a skeptic who wanted to prove that God doesn't exist. But guess what? He couldn't.

One of the reasons is a question Rev. Harber came up with about Christian martyrs: Why would they be willing to die for their faith? His answer is, simply, that they believed the gospel is true. Rev. Harber points out:

> Many people have died for a cause they believed was true even though it was false; however, no one ever eagerly dies for a cause knowing it to be false. Christianity could have never endured had these first Christians not believed in the Resurrection. The tenacity of these early eyewitness in the face of death testifies to the truth that the Resurrection must have occurred.[14]

Just Ask the Ones Who Saw Him

At the time the apostle Paul wrote his letters, many people who had seen the risen Lord were still alive (1 Corinthians 15:6). Paul told doubters to ask them what they had seen. Those who saw Christ were changed and were willing to die rather than to say they had not seen Jesus alive after His crucifixion. The ones who died for their faith would have only had to say, "Jesus is dead," and they could have lived.

Many Bad Ways to Die

With the exception of John (and Judas, who committed suicide after betraying Jesus), every one of the disciples was martyred in a terrible way and so were many other early Christians:

- Paul and Matthew were beheaded;
- Barnabas was burned;
- Mark was dragged to death;
- James, the Less, was clubbed to death;
- Peter, Philip, and Andrew were crucified;
- Thomas was speared;
- Luke was hung by the neck until dead;
- Stephen was stoned.

It is believed that Peter was crucified upside down at his own request because he thought himself "unworthy" to be crucified in the same way his Lord had been.

Would these men die for something they knew to be a lie or a trick they had played by stealing the body of Jesus? Even if one or two were determined to "stick to their story," it is not reasonable to think all of them would have died rather than admit to the lie. The obvious conclusion is that the eyewitnesses to Jesus' resurrection told what they believed to be true and refused to change their story, even in the face of terrible persecution, torture, and death. As author Tim LaHaye puts it, "They signed their testimony in blood."

Believe Them Because They Believed Enough to Die

One of the strongest arguments for the resurrection is that many people were willing to die because they insisted that Jesus is alive. The disciples knew Jesus Christ was God. They knew He was alive and well after being crucified. They walked, talked, and ate meals with Him. The disciples saw and touched the nail prints in His hands and the spear wound in Jesus' side, and they watched Him ascend into heaven.

The disciples were willing to be killed because it would have been a real lie for them to say that Jesus Christ was dead. They loved their Lord more than life and fully believed in what they had seen. They knew He had died for them, and now they were willing to die in order to proclaim Jesus as the sinless, risen Savior of the world.

Pray This: Thank the Lord Jesus Christ for the many faithful Christians who have been willing to die rather than deny that the resurrection is true. Ask the Lord Jesus to deepen your faith in Him and His resurrection.

What Do You Think?

1. Before becoming a follower of Jesus Christ, Pastor Frank Harber was a critic of Christianity. What was one compelling fact that convinced Frank that Christianity and the life, death, burial, and resurrection of Jesus Christ are true?

2. If the disciples of Jesus Christ wanted to keep from being killed, all they had to do was say what?

3. Standing for Biblical truth and opposing a lie may sometimes cost a Christian his or her _____.

12

DEFENDING AND CONTENDING FOR JESUS

Even if no one has yet tried to tell you that the Bible isn't true, it will happen sooner or later. Some people don't believe in God and try to make others doubt Him, too. One of their favorite ways to do that is to say the Bible sometimes contradicts itself (that means it says two different things happened when only one can possibly be true). Some "professional" skeptics point to what they say are 800 different contradictions in the Bible. If you look closely at each one, though, you can see clearly that there are no real contradictions. Let me give you a few examples of how this works.

Did Judas Die Two Different Ways?

The book of Matthew tells that, after betraying Jesus, Judas committed suicide by hanging himself (Matthew

27:5). And in Acts, it says Judas fell off a cliff and "burst open in the middle and all his entrails gushed out" (Acts 1:18). Do these two accounts conflict with each other? No, it is possible for both to be true, and it's easy to see how.

At the place in Jerusalem where Judas died, a cliff hangs over an open field. As a result, there are several possibilities as to what happened to Judas' body after he hanged himself:

1. It rotted and fell apart, landing in the field below the cliff; or
2. Someone came along, cut it down, and his body dropped from the cliff into the field; or
3. The rope or limb eventually broke, and the body fell into the field.

How Many Angels Did You Say Were There?

Here's another example. Matthew and Mark report that when the women went to the tomb of Jesus on resurrection morning, an angel was there. The gospels of Luke and John both say there were *two* angels at the tomb. Do these stories contradict each other? No, for two very good reasons. First, it is quite possible that one of the women later told the disciples she saw one angel while the other woman mentioned that she had seen two. It is also likely that one writer focused only on the angel who talked to the women while the other writer added information to the story by mentioning that one of the women saw two angels, one of which may have remained silent.

There is nothing wrong with two or more people reporting things differently. It happens every day in the news we read and hear about current events. I'll give you an example from my own experience.

Two Reporters, Two Stories

Actor Kirk Cameron has spoken at several of my Worldview Weekend conferences. If two newspaper reporters were to show up to tell about the Worldview Weekend, you would likely read two newspaper articles that each mention different facts about what went on. Yet they would not necessarily contradict each other.

If one reporter gives a summary of Mr. Cameron's remarks but does not mention that I was sitting in a chair on the side of the stage, and the other reporter writes that Brannon Howse was sitting in a chair on stage to the left of the speaker, does that reporter's story contradict the first one? Of course not. The two writers simply chose to emphasize different facts about what happened. In truth, the fact that the stories differ in some of the details actually substantiates the reports. It would be strange if both stories were exactly the same. That could imply that one reporter wasn't actually present and simply got all of his or her facts from the other reporter.

To come back to our example about the women at the tomb: While one of the gospels records that there was an angel at the tomb on resurrection morning, it does not say "there was *only one* angel at the tomb." So the accounts that mention one angel at the tomb and the accounts that mention two angels at the tomb do not contradict each other.

800 Ways Not to Be Wrong

Remember, the Judas and resurrection stories are only two of more than 800 such "contradictions" skeptics use to try and discredit the Bible. Each of the supposed errors can be readily explained by a reasonable interpretation of the events reported in Scripture.

We can use this kind of knowledge to defend the truth of the Bible and Christianity. After all, defending Biblical truth is not an option for Christians but a command from the Lord Jesus Christ Himself. In 1 Peter 3:15 we are told to "always be ready to give a defense to everyone who asks you a reason for the hope that is in you." Jude 3 says "to contend earnestly for the faith." And in

2 Corinthians 10:5 Paul tells us we should be "casting down arguments and every high thing that exalts itself against the knowledge of God, bringing every thought into captivity to the obedience of Christ."

I'll tell you one other advantage of being able to defend your faith: Knowing how to do it can also be a lot of fun.

Pray This: Thank the Lord God that the Bible is rich in stories and eyewitness accounts of God at work and that the way these reports are written give us good reasons to believe. Ask the Lord Jesus to help you understand how they all fit together.

What Do You Think?

1. While some people who oppose Christianity try to make it look as though the Bible contradicts itself, the Bible is really a complete and accurate revelation from beginning to _____.

2. True or false: Because one gospel writer gives different details from another means that one of their stories is wrong.

3. True or false: Christians should always be ready to defend the accuracy of the Bible.

A Closing Story

Jonathan Edwards:
How One Man's Faith
Shaped Generations of People

As my friend Dr. Marshall Foster says:

> We can all leave a 200-year footprint if we so de-
> sire. We each one of us, right now, whether we
> know it or not, stand at the apex of an unfold-
> ing generational drama. We are heir to the past,
> and ancestor to the future. Counting our grand-
> parents or early mentors, through our children
> and grandchildren, we will most likely mentor
> or be mentored by people whose life cycles will
> extend well over 200 years and include parts of
> four centuries.

Jonathan Edwards was one of the greatest preachers
of all time. He married a Christian lady named Sarah in

1727. They had a family of 11 children and are an example of two people who built a godly family that affected the world in amazing ways for more than a century:

> ...173 years after their marriage, a study was made of some 1,400 of their descendants. By 1900 this single marriage had produced 13 college presidents, 65 professors, 100 lawyers, a dean of an outstanding law school, 30 judges, 56 physicians, a dean of a medical school, 80 holders of public office, 3 United States senators, 3 mayors of large American cities, 3 governors, 1 vice president of the United States, 1 comptroller of the United States Treasury.
>
> Members of the family had written 135 books, edited 18 journals and periodicals. They had entered the ministry in platoons, with nearly 100 of them becoming missionaries overseas.[15]

Even though you're young now, by becoming a follower of Jesus Christ with a heart and mind strong for Him, you, too, can start making a lasting difference in the world!

NOTES

[1] Tripp, Tedd, *Shepherding a Child's Heart*, (Wapwallopen, PA: Shepherd Press, 1995), p. 6.

[2] Ibid, p. 123

[3] Geisler, Norm and Peter Bocchino, *Unshakable Foundations*, (Minneapolis, MN: Bethany House, 2001), p. 358.

[4] Cahill, Mark, *One Thing You Can't Do In Heaven* (Atlanta, GA: 2002), pp. 131-36.

[5] Brown, Dr. Walter T. Jr., *In the Beginning*, (Phoenix, AZ: Center For Scientific Creation, 1989), p. 2.

[6] Harber, Dr. Frank, *Reasons for Believing: A Seeker's Guide to Christianity* (Green Forest, AR: New Leaf Press, 1998), pp. 29-30.

[7] McDowell, Josh and Bob Hostetler, *Beyond Belief to Convictions* (Wheaton, IL: Tyndale House, 2002), p. 54

[8] Lutzer, Erwin, *Christ Among Other Gods* (Chicago: Moody Press, 1994), pp. 62-64.

[9] Geisler, Norm and Peter Bocchino, *Unshakable Foundations*, (Minneapolis, MN: Bethany House, 2001), p. 302.

[10] LaHaye, Dr. Tim, *Jesus Who is He?* (Sisters, Oregon: Multnomah Books, 1996), pp. 178

[11] Geisler, Norm and Peter Bocchino, *Unshakable Foundations*, (Minneapolis, MN: Bethany House, 2001), p. 302.

[12] *Master's Seminary Journal 8* (1997; 2002), 222.

[13] McDowell, Josh, *The Resurrection Factor* (Nashville: Thomas Nelson Publishers, 1981), pp. 6, 8.

[14] Harber, Dr. Frank, *Reason for Believing* (Green Forrest, AR: New Leaf Press, 1998), pp. 119-20.

[15] Foster, Dr. Marshall, co-author *No Retreats, No Reserves, No Regrets*, (Stewart House Press, 2000,) p.11.

ABOUT THE AUTHOR

Brannon Howse is president and founder of American Family Policy Institute and Worldview Weekend, America's largest Christian worldview conference series. Founded in 1993, Worldview Weekend is now held in seventeen states each year with an annual attendance of approximately 20,000. Brannon is also:

- Founder of www.christianworldviewnetwork.com, which features columns and articles by some of America's best Christian worldview authors and speakers.

- Founder of Worldview Weekend Online Institute (www.worldviewtraining.com), a 12-week online course exploring the Biblical worldview. The course is also available as in-class curriculum featuring leader and student manuals, DVDs, CDs, and tests.

- A trained tenor soloist who has sung in hundreds of American churches as well as at the Anaheim Convention Center for 10,000 delegates of the Association of Christian Schools International.

- Host of the Worldview Weekend Family Reunion held in Branson, Missouri, each spring and attended by more than 2,000 people. The three-day event features nationally known speakers, comedians, and musicians.

- Has conducted research for the White House Office of Faith Based Ministries as well as for best-selling authors Michael Reagan, Josh McDowell, and David Limbaugh.

- The education reporter and frequent guest host for *The Michael Reagan Show*.

- Author of five books on education, family issues, and Christianity, including *An Educational Abduction, Reclaiming A Nation At Risk* and *One Nation Under Man?: The Worldview War Between Christians and the Secular Left*.

- **President of Worldview Weekend Publishing.**

- Co-host of *Christian Worldview This Week*, a weekly radio broadcast heard on more than 225 stations each week.

- Has apppeared on over 600 radio and television programs, including *The O'Reilly Factor* (Fox News), *The News on MSNBC, Truths That Transform with Dr. D. James Kennedy, The G. Gordon Liddy Show, The Michael Reagan Show, The Ken Hamblin Show, The Oliver North Show, Action Sixties, Point of View, Family News and Focus, U.S.A. Radio News,* and *Standard News*.

ABOUT WORLDVIEW
WEEKEND CONFERENCES

Christians today are bombarded with information and opinions by the media, schools, and government. No one can hope to assimilate the avalanche of data. So who could possibly understand the times in which we live? Not many! But those men and women who do become the next generation of leaders.

The Bible speaks of a small tribe in Israel that "had understanding of the times" and knew "what Israel ought to do," and, as a result, they became leaders (1 Chronicles 12:32). God expects His people to seek earnestly for the truth, rewarding with greater responsibility those who comprehend. Worldview Weekend Conferences are dedicated to teaching you how to understand our times and grasp the opportunity that will give you for leadership.

Worldview Weekend features nationally known speakers such as Josh McDowell, David Limbaugh, David Barton, Kirk Cameron, David Jeremiah, Kerby Anderson, Star Parker, Al Denson, Erwin Lutzer, and others. U.S. Congressman Tom DeLay has been a keynote speaker at Worldview Weekend, as well as the Honorable Dick Armey when he was U.S. House Majority Leader.

To find out more about how to attend the Worldview Weekend of your choice, go to www.worldviewweekend.com.

Worldview Weekend Resources

We invite you to take advantage of these helpful
Worldview Weekend Resources:

- Visit worldviewweekend.com and check out the **Berean Club.**
  You can load more than 125 Worldview Weekend keynote
  presentations onto your ipod, listen online or burn a cd.

- Further your worldview knowledge by taking our online
  course, **Developing a Christian Worldview.** Try our free demo
  at worldviewtraining.com

- We have DVDs featuring *Kirk Cameron, Ray Comfort, David Barton,
  Josh McDowell, Sean McDowell* and others. Check out our books
  and DVDs in our bookstore at worldviewweekend.com

- Visit christianworldviewnetwork.com for daily news and
  columns from a Biblical worldview perspective.

- Brannon's book, *One Nation Under Man? The Worldview War
  Between Christians and the Secular Left*, can be purchased
  from our online bookstore at worldviewweekend.com.